RUGBY UNION

Ken Adwick: Golf
Chester Barnes: Table Tennis
Bill Berry: Water-Skiing
John Cadman & W. van Heumen: Indoor Hockey
Henry Cooper: Boxing
John Dawes: Rugby Union
Richard Hawkey: Squash Rackets
Rachel Heyhoe Flint: Women's Hockey
Brian Jacks: Judo
Jack Karnehm: Understanding Billiards and Snooker
John Le Masurier & Denis Watts: Athletics — Track Events
Howard & Rosemary Payne: Athletics — Throwing
Barry Richards: Cricket
Bill Scull: Gliding and Soaring
Denis Watts: Athletics — Jumping and Vaulting
Paul and Sue Whetnall: Badminton
Peter Williams: Canoeing
Bob Wilson: Soccer

Pelham Pictorial Sports Instruction Series

John Dawes
RUGBY UNION

Pelham  Books

Picture Credits:
Tony Duffy: 1, 5—7, 11, 22—6, 29, 31—4, 36
Mel Davies: 2—4, 8—10, 12—21, 27—8, 30, 35, 42—65
George Herringshaw: 37—41

First published in Great Britain by
PELHAM BOOKS LTD
44 Bedford Square
London WC1B 3DU
April 1975
Second impression July 1980

1975 John Dawes

ISBN 0 7207 0792 7

Printed in Singapore

Contents

Introduction

There have been many books written far and wide about rugby football and the coaching of it. Many of these are thoroughly worthwhile and enjoyable, while others are purely technical and sometimes difficult to digest – especially for the newcomer to rugby football.

This book has been written not in a pure technical sense (although in fact it was desperately difficult at times not to be), but more in a readable, 'look and learn' sense. It is, therefore, hoped that it will be of help to anyone interested in playing rugby football, whether for the first time or for the thousandth time.

The illustrations used have been chosen because they attempt to capture in black and white that particular skill of a particular player which excites thousands of sportsmen throughout the world. Most have been selected from game situations, because when a situation is specially set up it often loses some of the vital ingredients and may not reflect how that particular player performs on the field of play. Gerald Davies, for example, when asked to show a side-step or swerve to a group of youngsters, had to stop and think for several moments on what he did. It was quite amusing to follow him around the field as he tried to analyse his own side-step and swerve.

Many of the skills illustrated, therefore, in this book, are purely instinctive and very difficult consciously to reproduce for a demonstration. Nevertheless, in looking at the photographs there might be some aspect which the reader can spot and then try to improve that aspect of his own play.

On the other hand, much of what is shown are aspects which can be practised and utilised by a team. After all, we cannot all be a Gerald Davies or a Mike Gibson or a David Duckham; but we can improve our play to enable players with these skills to get the ball in their hands.

With regard to the essential forward play characteristics of the game, that is, the scrum, line-out and so on, no attempt has been made to be ultra-technical; for example, describing how a prop forward should place his feet in positions X and Y at the set scrummage. Instead, a rather broader viewpoint has been taken with some of the essential features mentioned, together with the individual attributes needed by a forward in a particular position.

Rugby Union

There has been a conscious attempt throughout to regard all players alike while, of course, recognising that because of physical size, strength and temperament, certain players are best suited to certain positions. If as a result a prop forward is more aware of the need to be able to give and take a pass, or a centre more conscious of his decisive role in a ruck or maul, then writing the book will have been worthwhile. Further, players of all ages and ability might realise how essential it is to practise with and without colleagues, if the game is going to be worthwhile and enjoyable.

CHAPTER ONE

The Pass

Ever since William Webb Ellis picked up a football on the playing-fields of Rugby School in 1823, rugby football has been essentially a handling game. It is easy to experience the frustrations of players and spectators alike, therefore, when the game breaks down because this particular aspect is badly executed. Yet this is the one skill at which, with a great deal of patience and constant practice, every player can reach a standard sufficient to play a game which will then be worthwhile and enjoyable.

Passing, of course, can take various forms and involve several different techniques, but in the final analysis it is the ability of one player to transfer the ball to a colleague accurately, and in such a way as to ensure the probability of its being caught. Having made such a statement there are, however, certain types of passes which are fundamental and ensure continuity. These are the passes which can, and ought to be, practised regularly. Practice in passing develops one's own confidence to such an extent that when the relevant situation arises during a game, the player makes the appropriate pass without apparently being conscious of the technique involved.

However, whichever technique is employed, the resulting pass is judged by the following criteria :

(a) it must be accurate ;
(b) it must be made so that the ball travels at the correct speed ;
(c) it must be delivered at the right time.

All three criteria are equally important because failure in any one aspect can make a pass ineffective. For a pass to be ACCURATE it must be placed comfortably in front of the receiver. While this will, of course, vary with the running aspect of the passer and the receiver, the ball must reach the receiver's hands at a height which enables him to kick or pass the ball further, or to continue running, with the minimum of adjustment.

If the pass is WELL TIMED it will enable the receiver to decide his next course of action more confidently. A badly timed pass can place a colleague in great difficulty irrespective of how accurate it is. Similarly, a pass delivered too hard makes the catching of the ball more difficult, whereas too slow a pass

Rugby Union

can place the receiver under the most severe pressure.

How annoying it is for a team to be involved in a thrilling movement covering sixty yards or so, only to see the scoring pass fail to reach its target because of inaccuracy or bad timing.

There are many types of passing which occur during a game, these are illustrated below. The requisite skills in giving these passes can be acquired by all players with practice.

The Dive Pass

This illustration shows Gareth Edwards in a very spectacular dive pass. It is obvious that he is totally committed to the pass and completely oblivious to pressure from opponents or the fact that he is going to hit the ground with a 'bump'. This is the type of pass that scrum-halves are forced to use when under the severest pressure to get the ball to a colleague as quickly as possible. The advantages of it are speed and length, but a disadvantage is that it does result in the scrum-half being prostrate on the ground, and hence temporarily 'out of the game'.

10

The Scissors

This sequence shows the author and Mike Gibson demonstrating the scissors pass. The essentials are as follows :

(*a*) both players must keep their eyes on the ball at all times ;

(*b*) delivery must be perfectly timed ;

(*c*) the *receiver* must see the ball at all times and never at any time be in a position where the ball cannot be seen ;

(*d*) the running of both players must be perfectly timed ;

(*e*) each player must have complete faith in the other's ability – the outcome of constant practice.

Rugby Union
The Quick Pass

This is very much a high-pressure pass which is used in an attempt to speed up the movement of the ball between at least three players. The 1971 Lions relied a great deal on this particularly, and the rewards were to see Gerald Davies or David Duckham scoring several tries. If it is to be attempted, the player who is actually going to make the quick pass must RECEIVE the ball perfectly. It MUST be placed out in front of him at a comfortable distance. Secondly, he must be confident that the player who is going to receive the ball from him is in the correct position. Then it is a simple matter of transferring one's hands (with the ball) in one CONTINUOUS movement (contrast the momentarily static position of the ball in the normal three-quarter pass) from left to right, or vice versa. If done quickly enough, the impression is given that the ball is NOT held, but this is not so, otherwise inaccuracy would result. It is not a 'pat-' or 'flick-on'.

Conventional Three-quarter Pass

These two illustrations taken from the England–Ireland game in 1974 show Tony Ensor about to deliver the perfect pass. Notice the position of his body is totally committing the tackler, and such is his timing, speed and accuracy in delivering the final pass that Mike Gibson simply had to catch the ball to score, which of course he did.

Rugby Union

Spin Pass

These illustrations show Sid Going practising a spin pass and Lyn Collinge actually using it during a game. Both photographs show that the feet are well apart ; that the hand producing the spin is the right hand ; and the centre of gravity of the body is low. It is the follow-through and not the 'wind-up' which is important in this type of pass.

When to use a spin pass is a matter of judgement, but it does require more room than the normal scrum-half pass, and therefore is mostly used at line-outs, rucks and mauls. At the set scrummage a scrum-half usually finds that he is under pressure to get the ball away quickly. The advantage of the spin pass, of course, is the greater length it obtains. Gareth Edwards can pass consistently during a game a distance of 25 yards or so. This must give the fly-half an advantage over his opponents.

14

The Short Support Pass

This is a pass more often than not employed by the forwards. It is a pass made IMMEDIATELY AFTER or ON contact with an opponent. The essential feature is to 'drive through' an opponent, completely committing him to the tackle and yet 'leaving the ball behind' for a close-supporting colleague.

15

Rugby Union

Conclusion

There are many other types of unorthodox passes which from time to time feature in a game. The most popular among these are the reverse pass, the torpedo pass and the overhead pass, as illustrated.

The most important aspect of any pass is transference of the ball with accuracy, timing and speed. It matters 'nought' how pretty it looks – only how effective it is.

CHAPTER TWO

The Kick

Although the game of rugby football is essentially a handling game, many matches (perhaps too many) are won or lost because of kicking. Every team should possess an accurate place kicker because of the number of opportunities to kick at goal which present themselves in every match. So numerous are these opportunities that a poor side possessing a good place kicker may beat a good side without one. Although place kicking collects the points, tactical kicking has an equally important role to play and every player should be competent at it.

Kicking should not be looked upon purely as a means of getting out of trouble. It is the easiest way of gaining ground either in defence or attack. The main disadvantage is that one cannot retain the degree of control that one has with the ball in the hands.

As in passing, accuracy is a key factor. A misdirected kick can have disastrous consequences. A well-placed kick can gain territorial advantage or lead directly to a try, whereas a badly-aimed kick surrenders possession and gives the opponents a chance to counter-attack.

The good kicker must have every type of kick at his disposal and the judgement to use the right kick in the right situation. Whereas judgement comes with experience, the skills of kicking can, and will, only be attained by constant practice. (For example, Phil Bennett will not start training until, while standing at the corner flag, he is able to screw kick the ball between the goal-posts four times.)

Undoubtedly the most used kick in the actual game is the punt, illustrated here by Phil Bennett and Gareth Edwards. Although each of these players have different individual techniques certain factors are common to both. Notice, for example, how perfectly *balanced* they are at the moment of impact ; this ensures that the ball goes in the right direction and allows the kicker to apply the correct power. Look next at the care each player takes when *holding the ball* just before the kick. It is no coincidence that they hold the ball in a similar fashion. To be able to adjust to this position quickly during a game is important to the success of the kick. The other important factor (which is common to all ball skills) is that their *eyes are never taken off the ball* until it is well on its way and the follow-through is completed. The follow-

through helps both direction and power. What has made these players great kickers is that they have always kicked this way, even when subjected to enormous pressure during matches. Furthermore, they were able to strike the ball equally well with either foot although neither were naturally two-footed. This versatility was only achieved after a great deal of practice. One often sees a one-footed player in all sorts of trouble because of this failing.

The drop kick requires the concentration on the same factors as the punt, i.e. balance, holding the ball correctly, eyes on the ball and follow-through, but the method of holding the ball assumes even greater importance

because by definition the ball must be struck on the half volley. This can be illustrated by the study of the following photographs of Mike Gibson. So technically perfect is this drop kick that it is difficult to believe it is not a place kick. Notice the care with which the ball is dropped prior to impact and compare the body posture in drop kicking to that in the punt.

Place kicking differs to the punt and drop kick in that the ball is not in the hand. Once again, however, most of the same factors apply. The method of holding the ball is not relevant but placement of the ball requires the same amount of care. The average time, for

Rugby Union

example, taken by Bob Hiller during a game is 55 seconds, but his success rate justifies it totally. These two kicks by Bob Hiller are so consistent that it could be argued that they are different photographs of the same kick. One has to count the number of studs on the

boot to verify that they are not. Whichever of these styles is employed depends upon the individual. Although there are many technical arguments about the styles, the prolific goal-kicking feats of Bob Hiller and Phil Bennett justify their own individual styles.

CHAPTER THREE

Running

Although many forwards would prefer the game to be 'semi-static' in order that their reputed strength may be utilised to maximum extent without the effort of having 'to get there' – running is an essential part of the game of rugby football. When looking at the modern players, who can fail to thrill to the sight of Gerald Davies or David Duckham in full cry ? Without doubt these are two of the most gifted runners in world rugby, and yet inevitably the question arises 'Can I hope to become a Gerald Davies or a David Duckham ?'

Certainly such running ability as is evident in these two players is a gift from 'up-above', but a certain amount can be done by analysis and practice. The qualities exhibited by these two players are obviously innate, but they can be compartmentalised and therefore taught and learned. Whether or not the judgement of when to use these running skills can be taught is a matter for conjecture.

However the basic skills of running necessarily incur speed, change of pace, balance and change of direction.

Speed is one aspect of running which can be improved by the individual. If a player is looking for ways to increase his speed, whether over a short or long distance, then most of his running practices ought to be done wearing spiked running shoes. Then simply by repetitive sprints he will gradually increase basic speed, although it may take rather a lengthy period of time before any noticeable increase is observed. Patience and practice are the key words here to improve basic speed.

Of course running with a rugby ball in the hand is far different from a straightforward fifty-yard dash. An essential attribute here is balance, but once again this can be mastered via practice. There are two ways of carrying a rugby ball – in one hand or in both. Whichever is employed is determined by the intentions of the ball carriers.

The following illustrations show Gerald Davies, David Duckham and Alan Richards in full cry, carrying the ball one-handed.

It is obvious from these illustrations that Gerald, David and Alan are 'haring' for the line and that at this particular moment in time each player has set his sights on the try line and to score a try is his objective.

Rugby Union

Now study the following illustrations of John Bevan, Gareth Edwards and the author running while holding the ball two-handed.

Equally so the players shown here using two hands are running with the intention of passing at some stage to another player. The ball held in this way makes it fairly simple to pass to the right or to the left. Carrying the ball in this way does, however, effect the speed of the runner. Maximum speed is usually attained when carrying the ball cradled in one arm as in the illustrations above.

Change of pace is really a matter of deceiving the would-be tackler and it is judgement of when to slow down and then quickly accelerate which is the most difficult aspect. Experience can only teach this, but the player must have the confidence to try it.

Of course the side-step and swerve are the two most exciting aspects of the running skills, and as can be seen from the photos below it is largely a question of balance.

The ball is carried by the players in a way which helps their balance — in the right arm when side-stepping off the right foot, and left arm for left foot. Although difficult to see in a photograph the thrust off the appropriate foot is both powerful and vicious, in many cases accompanied by a lessening in speed. A side-step can of course be practised, but it is knowing *when* to use it in a match situation which makes it devastating. Many side-steps fail because the player misreads the position of his opponent and would-be tackler. It is essential for the opponent to be 'set-up', that is, to make him believe that you are going to

run one way and then sharply and incisively change that direction before he has time to recover.

The swerve is another running technique which, when perfectly executed, can be most rewarding. Again the way the ball is carried is an important factor because in this balance is crucial.

There is no sharp thrust from the ground in this case, but look at the way the body (especially the hips) is evading the clasp of the tackler.

The skills of running are not complex but for them to be mastered and hence most profitably employed during a match then many hours must be spent on the practice ground.

Unless, of course, you are a Gerald Davies, a David Duckham, or a Mike Gibson!

Rugby Union

In this sequence Gerald Davies performs a sharp thrust of his right foot which leaves the would-be tackler helpless, only to encounter a defender who is covering. An attempted hand-off is only partially successful, but the awareness of the player is apparent because the ball is passed to a support player and a try results.

The classic side step, demonstrated by Mike Gibson.

This illustrates that David Duckham, having feinted to go outside J. Karam (New Zealand), produces a devastating thrust off his left foot which takes him inside and past Karam. This technique also applies on the Mike Gibson sequence.

This sequence taken from the 1974 England–Ireland game shows the effect of a dummy and a side-step by Mike Gibson. The dummy causes the ball to be held in the wrong arm for the left foot thrust, but such is Gibson's balance that the side-step is effective.

Not only are the hips (the tackle target) well away from the would-be tackler, but look at the incline of John Bevan's body. This could only be maintained at speed.

31

CHAPTER FOUR

Physical Contact

Physical contact can be the most difficult part of rugby to get used to for the young (or not so young) player taking up the game for the first time. It is a glorious sight to see John Williams stop a man in full flight but it is not only courage that is involved but a great deal of skill. Many a young convert to rugby has been completely 'put off' the game before really getting to grips with it because he has been hurt making a tackle. This is nothing to do with being brave – nobody enjoys being hurt – and being brave does not make a good tackler, although it helps.

Almost as many people who give up do so because of being hurt while being tackled. Taking a tackle, or better still warding off a tackle, is just as much a skill as tackling.

There are other physical contact situations which occur in the scrum, line-out, ruck and maul but these are dealt with in chapters devoted to those unit skills. We shall devote this chapter to the individual in a body contact situation. There is one main principle which is the same whether going into another player with the ball or without it – to make the ball available for your own team after impact.

Obviously there are times when tackling when the player is content to stop his opposition without gaining the ball for his team but even then he should be thinking about ways of turning the situation to the advantage of his team.

There are other subsidiary principles which help to achieve this aim whether carrying the ball or stopping the ball carrier :

(1) hit the other player harder than he hits you ;
(2) think of the position of the ball.

Tackling

Tackling is one of the most difficult skills to master, but, once mastered, becomes second nature and one of the easiest. There are many ways of tackling a player :
The really good tackler will employ all these skills and more because he cannot always get into the perfect position. To use the right tackle at the right time is almost as important as making the tackle at all. It is pointless crash tackling the ball carrier if he has time to pass the ball. You take yourself

out of the game as well as him and he has completed his function in that movement.

However, there are certain points which any tackler should try to follow whenever possible :

(1) He should try to make first contact with his shoulder.

(2) He should always pull himself as close to his quarry as possible. This ensures that (*a*) he is in a strong position to hold on to his opponent until the ball is relaxed ; (*b*) he is not hurt by his opponent bursting

through him or caught by flying arms and legs.

(3) He should prevent the ball carrier from running by taking his legs. The obvious exception to this is in the smother tackle, when the

priority is to prevent the pass and therefore the arms are pinned. Similarly the head-on tackle on your own try line must be made higher to knock the man backwards.

Rugby Union

Rugby Union

Look at this series of photographs from the Wales *v.* France match in 1972. Gerald Davies here proves what a fine defensive player he is in addition to his known skills in attack. Notice how he gets his hand on the ball and then throws all his weight into turning his man over on to his back. Not only can the Frenchman not ground the ball, but he cannot pass either, and has to take it into touch. The flag which can be seen in the last picture is the corner flag, so this tackle saved a try. Any normal textbook tackle would not have succeeded.

Running into a Tackle

In this situation a player always has to balance trying to run through the tackle with securing the ball for his own side if tackled. Nothing is more frustrating to a team than to see a winger make sixty yards, run into the last man and knock the ball forward. Body position and position of the ball are all important.

In this picture John Williams is first trying to drive the tackler out of his way. He puts himself in a strong position (which also helps to prevent injury) and leads with his shoulder while keeping the ball firmly away from contact so that if tackled he leaves it available for his own support.

In a close-contact situation involving several players (more usual in the forwards than the backs but just as important for a back if he finds himself in that situation) exactly the same principles apply but it is more important to try to remain standing and even more important to keep the ball away from the opposition. You can see from these photographs that the movement in each case should continue because the ball is available to the support player.

37

The final word in this chapter again belongs to Gerald Davies, showing superb control on the tackle in a match against Ireland. Gareth Edwards has supported his run, and on the tackle Gerald Davies releases the ball perfectly to give him a scoring pass.

CHAPTER FIVE

Positional Play

The preceding chapters have dealt with the skills and techniques which ALL players should possess. Too often in the past, especially in British rugby, the attitude has been that one does not expect a big powerful heavy lock forward to run and pass like a three-quarter – but merely to fulfil his role as a ball-winner. Yet this statement is refuted immediately when one thinks of those giants among lock forwards, Frik du Preez (South Africa) and Colin Meads (New Zealand). A closer analysis of these two players shows that as well as being immensely powerful and efficient in their specialist roles, they also possess a high degree of skill in the other attributes hitherto not associated with men who play in their positions. This surely is how it should be for all players. Each player participating in the game should reach a reasonable standard in skills and techniques – a standard such that if physical characteristics were discounted, it would be difficult to identify a player with a particular position. Give Barry John or Gerald Davies another six or so stones and who is to say that they would not have made international forwards?

Nevertheless, a player in a certain position is often identifiable by the way he exhibits a certain skill. This will perhaps become apparent when the following descriptions of the fifteen players are read.

The Full-back

First and foremost this player is your last line of defence and must above all other qualities exhibit courage, safe hands and a strong tackle. The ability to kick and counter-attack are really bonuses to a team although it is the player who possesses most of these who reaches the top grade. As in all positions weight and size are an added advantage but are not necessarily essential qualities.

The Wings

Wings, both right and left, have to possess the one basic commodity – speed. In the chapter dealing with three-quarter play, it is emphasised that the duty of midfield players is to try and let the wings receive the ball early so that maximum space may be utilised. Speed, therefore, is an essential attribute in order to make best use of the situation produced by the three-quarter line. This does not, of course, mean for one moment that other attributes are unimportant : a good pair of hands (it means a great deal in confidence to a centre if he knows that whatever he passes out is caught) ; a strong tackle ; good positional sense ; and the ability to swerve, side-step and kick.

There is one other aspect concerning the wings that the advent of the attacking full-back has demanded. The blind side wing must always be in a position to cover the unavoidable gap left by a full-back committed to attack. This requires no more than concentration and awareness — there is no player better than David Duckham at this.

Finally, it should always be remembered that left wing is a very different position from right wing. It is not a simple transference from right to left — it requires patience, hard work and plenty of practice — seldom does it happen overnight !

The Centres (or Midfield)

These days more than ever the two centres and fly-half are developing into a *midfield UNIT* and at long last the idea of three talented players playing in midfield as individuals is being abandoned. More than ever, the understanding between these three is both essential and crucial to a team. Whether in attack or defence, it helps enormously to agree on different positional tactics. For example, there might be a conscious attempt to change the line of defence thus making it more difficult for the opposition's

attack.

It is extremely difficult in modern rugby to crash tackle in the centre especially when the opposition have won good ball. As a result of training and practising together, it is now possible for the midfield unit to shepherd the opposition into a particular situation and then strike effectively. While it is essential for a player to possess the obvious individual qualities this type of defence is developed by great understanding and compatibility.

In attack, it is vital that the midfield have the skill to transfer the ball very quickly especially from set pieces. This has been dealt with on the chapter on three-quarter play.

The Fly-Half

This is probably the most crucial position behind the scrum, if not the whole team. As well as being required to possess *all* the individual skills to a greater degree than another player, this position demands the one quality which can affect a team's performance — JUDGEMENT. This player has to decide, as soon as he receives the ball, whether to kick, pass or run ; and if he chooses wrongly, the progress of the team is halted. It is extremely difficult to instil judgement but it can be improved by the confidence a player derives from practising individual skills and working incessantly with the people with whom he is going to play. Barry John's judgement — perhaps even more than his individual skills — was certainly a major factor in the success of Wales and the British Lions in New Zealand in 1971.

Rugby Union
The Scrum-Half

Again without listing the individual qualities necessary to make a good scrum-half, three aspects are essential — COURAGE, FORTITUDE and COMPETITIVENESS. If one thinks of the world's top scrum-halves, then while they all possess scrum-half qualities, it is these three aspects which make them the world-class players they are. Names such as Gareth Edwards, Sid Going and Jan Webster substantially support this view.

Of course, the liaison between scrum-half and forwards, and scrum-half and three-quarters, is still an essential item in any team strategy, but this has not changed at all over the years. While there are many ways a scrum-half can play a game, it is the above qualities which are essential to ensure success.

The Flanker

He is the link between the backs and forwards, and which combination of forward and back attributes is most effective will depend upon the sort of game the team plays.

A slower, more powerful type of forward, who has immense penetration close to the scrum, is not going to be the best man to support play if the team relies on creating overlaps for its wingers. However, he must be first and foremost a forward with a commitment in that direction. He must also have great stamina as he will be expected to be in the centre of every piece of action.

Although it is no longer possible to crash tackle the fly-half each time he gets the ball, he must be particularly strong in this phase of play.

The No.8

His game is very closely linked with that of the flankers and he will need many of the same qualities. Normally he will be bigger, not just because of tradition but because this makes it easier to lock the scrum and a line-out man is needed at the back of the line-out. As the initiator of many attacks from the base of the scrum, he must have good hands.

He will also need immense courage as he is very often expected to fall on the ball to secure possession when it has gone loose from a tackler.

Second Row

Because of his size, he is not expected to be the most mobile player on the field, but to compensate for this he should be one of the strongest. The ability to rip a ball out from a man when the back row have managed almost to make it available is required. Similarly, having caught a line-out ball, he should be able to prevent himself from being robbed.

He must be able to trap. Many big men carry too much weight which prevents them from being effective in the line-out. There is no virtue in lighter weights unless they can be used.

Prop

He must have a back of iron. Traditionally the worst handler in the team, this should not be so and no prop should be content just to scrummage. Like the 2nd row, he needs enough power to get to the breakdown before the ball has gone and enough strength to make his presence tell. Any weakness in scrummaging will be reflected throughout the whole team so if needed extra strength training must be done out of season.

Hooker

The most underused member of the scrum. Because he has to be more supple and adaptable than the prop, a hooker is usually smaller. He should be mobile and able to work much more than is normally expected in the loose. In a tight scrum, his job is more than just to win the ball. As soon as it is won, he must add to the push and ensure that he wins good ball. On the opposition put-in, he must use his discretion as to when he should push or go for a strike. Far too many hookers count the score only in heads won and lost when it is points that count.

CHAPTER SIX

The Line-out

Although the line-out has been reduced in importance since the change in the law of kicking directly for touch, there are up to eighty in a match and it is therefore still an important source of first-phase possession. At the moment it is probably the most untidy phase of play and therefore the team which has good line-out techniques has an enormous advantage over the opposition.

The first and most important technique is throwing in. This still is often totally neglected and is performed so badly in the senior game that all the elaborate practices of special ploys to win the ball come to nothing in a game because the ball never reaches its intended target. Throwing the ball at the right speed and height for up to three jumpers is a skill which needs practising constantly, and whether it be a forward or a back who is given the task, he must spend time with those jumpers until he gets it right 90 per cent and not 40 per cent of the time.

Having mastered throwing the ball in straight, and at the right height and speed, one of the great problems is to protect the ball winner and receiver from opponents only too ready to pounce the

moment the ball has been won.

This means that there are really two choices. The first is to tap the ball accurately and quickly to the scrum-half, who will pass it equally quickly to move it away from marauding forwards.

If you look at the photographs on the right, the main thing to notice is how carefully the jumpers handle the ball. These pictures show how the fingers play an important part in accurately deflecting the ball. There is no question of swinging an arm and hoping to make contact. In the picture on page 46 Moss Keane of Ireland goes one stage further and uses two hands to offset the ball. The second is to catch it and then form a maul and release the ball when all the forwards on the other side have been committed and the scrum-half is safe.

The first sequence also illustrates the rough and tumble which a line-out often has to overcome despite law changes to try and keep the lines apart.

Occasionally the ball is won well enough to catch two-handed and pass while still at the peak of the jump.

The pictures on pages 47 and 48 show the two different types of two-handed

catch. Page 47 shows a low throw and the jumper is in a totally strong position so that he can distribute the ball having won it without being robbed by the opposition. This is only suitable at the front of the line-out. If it is attempted further back it will almost certainly be intercepted. The top left-hand picture on page 48 shows a high leap and the great problem is then to change the ball from that weak position to a strong position before he is robbed.

One way of overcoming this problem is to tap the ball down to a team-mate in

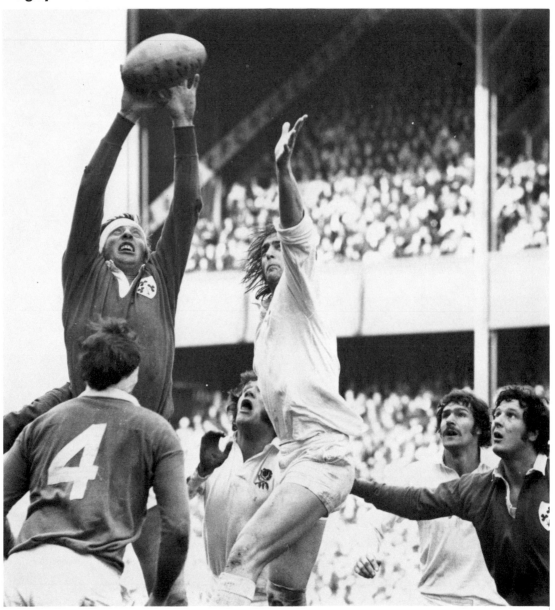

the line-out who will distribute it for the jumper.

So far the other forwards not involved in actually winning the ball have not been mentioned. Their task is almost more important than that of the jumper.

They must block all the holes as soon as the ball is won so that the jumper is not isolated or the scrum-half decapitated while receiving man and ball at the same time.

At the present time it is made more

difficult because players on the same side must stand a yard apart until the ball has been deflected or caught, but then they are allowed to support the man with the ball so it is still possible.

In the sequence overleaf, Alan Sutherland of New Zealand has caught the ball two-handed and brought it down into a strong position. His fellow forwards immediately move in to protect him and every chance of the opposition ruining the possession he has just won is eliminated. Notice how the Cambridge hand which could just prevent perfect delivery to the scrum-half is taken away.

Page 49 shows a less elegant but none the less effective example of 'blocking'. Mervyn Davies has won the ball and Ian Kirkpatrick is trying to get through to the scrum-half. John Taylor has bound just tight enough to keep him at bay. Meanwhile Peter Dixon and Delme Thomas have left no room in front.

The line-out is a unit still just like scrummaging and every man has a job to do. Once this is recognised and each individual can rely upon the other (including the thrower in), a team can begin to look forward to the prospect of a line-out instead of wondering what is

Rugby Union

going to happen.

All the thinking so far put forward in this chapter assumes that the size of the line-out forwards permits fairly orthodox tactics in the line-out. However, it may be that because no player of the right size is available there is a need to resort to more unorthodox tactics. This can involve shortening the line-out and throwing to the scrum-half over the top or to a powerful forward bursting on to it from ten yards back. It may alternatively involve throwing to the first man in the line-out.

It must be remembered that the line-out is only one aspect of play and if a side is really weak in that direction, but strong in others, it might even be tactically sound never to put the ball into touch. This will ensure that at least you always have control over the throw, and can therefore use ploys to offset obvious weaknesses.

CHAPTER SEVEN

The Scrummage

There are very powerful arguments for scrummaging to be recognised as the most important aspect of the game of rugby. There are obviously other important skills but many of them will never be put to the test if the ball is not first won at the scrummage.

On many tours it was recognised that the British Lions had far better attacking players behind the scrum and yet not until 1971 did they succeed in winning a tour. This was done mostly by working so hard on scrummaging that the All Blacks were completely outplayed. This resulted in opportunities for the back division to show their skills and put the New Zealand forwards in a defensive role at which they were not as impressive as when supporting movement going forward. Although the loose forward play of the Lions never matched that of the All Blacks such was the advantage created by better scrummaging that the series was won.

To emphasise the importance of the scrum it is worth noting that there are up to fifty in most games. Teams which can dominate the scrums can often win even if they are not playing good rugby after winning the ball. Often people refer to

ten-man rugby, which means a team wins the ball and uses its half-backs to kick for ground, never bringing the back division into play. Before the change of line-out laws this pattern of rugby was almost the only type seen at international level where there was a need to win at all costs.

Thankfully, the game is now much more attractive but the scrum remains absolutely important in gaining possession in the first instance.

All forwards whether in the back row or the front must be totally committed to the scrum. Although this seems obvious it cannot be repeated too much because it is very easy to use the scrum as a period of rest after some particularly vigorous and energy sapping loose play.

The whole formation of a scrum relies on all eight forwards and will become lopsided if one man is not doing his job. This results in an involuntary wheel which is not easy to control.

It can be seen from the pushing positions in Fig. 1 that every forward is needed to produce the forward thrust wanted.

Another underestimated ingredient of scrummaging is the binding. Eight

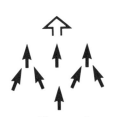

Figure 1

players locked together as one will find it very easy to hold eight individuals much bigger than themselves who are trying to move them without being bound together. It is even possible to move a scrum just by tightening the binding and without actually pushing. At the end of a match a forward's arms should be aching from trying to bind tighter at every scrum. There are two totally different situations in scrummaging :

(1) Your own 'put-in' ;
(2) The opposition's 'put-in'.

It is obvious at times that teams never sort out the difference because they go into scrums hooking for each ball no matter who is putting it in and no matter whether or not successful.

The scrum is a mini-team in itself and must work out its aims and ways of achieving them. Basically these are simple :

(1) To win good ball on your own put-in ;
(2) To win opposition ball if it can be done while still giving your side good ball ;
(3) To make bad ball for the opposition even though they win it.

The second point is important. It became fashionable at one time to play tight-head props who were expert hookers of opposition ball. To do this they would often contract themselves into very weak positions so that even when won the ball was useless. If not won it was a disaster as the prop could not transmit the push from the rest of scrum and therefore there was no chance of making bad ball for the opposition. The best opposition ball to win is the one not struck for but pushed for so that the opposition are pushed off the ball having hooked it. This automatically puts them at a disadvantage in defence as it is difficult to stay organised while moving backwards.

In the picture on page 52 it should be easy to tell which side is putting the ball in even if the scrum-half were removed from the shot. The dark shirts have adopted a locking position – legs straight with the 'we shall not be moved' thought uppermost in their minds. This means they just want to remain steady while the ball is hooked. The team in white are adopting a much more aggressive formation to try and push them off the ball. It should also be obvious from the photograph that they will not succeed. Look how high they are and look how the prop has been forced to arch his back.

It is not often that a scrummage will succeed in moving forward while hooking the ball on its own head and it is better not to try unless a back-row move is to be attempted. In this case forward momentum, however little, will improve the chances of success enormously. It not only gives the movement a start but also commits the opposition to stopping the retreat and therefore ties in the flankers. Even the scrum-half will be on

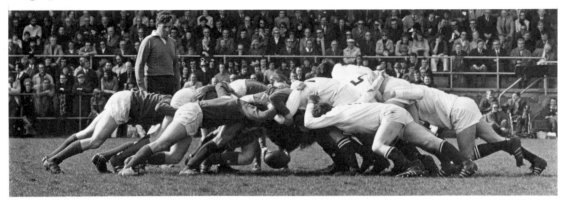

the retreat and therefore less effective in harrassing the movement.

The fashionable formation in the scrum is as shown in Fig. 1 but it is not the only one and should not be taken as such. If a back-row move is intended it might be profitable to move a flanker so that both are on the same side. This can also be done if wheeling the scrum is to be attempted. There is little point in having a player pack behind a prop who is going to pull instead of push. It can also place an extra man in a position to exploit the move.

There is even some point in thinking about varying the number of forwards going into a scrum. Gerwyn Williams argued that it was sensible to put up to twelve men in a scrum if going for a push-over try and confident of hooking it. Most teams are not willing to risk doing this but the idea is quite valid. On the opposite tack there is some merit in reducing the number in the scrum particularly if the opposition is pushing the scrum back at a rate of knots. This may appear contradictory but it is not.

If a scrum is being pushed (particularly if a forward is missing because he has been injured) it is difficult to heel the ball cleanly – even a good channel is difficult to keep under pressure. If the scrum is reduced to five or even three there are less legs in the way and therefore more chance of the ball being hooked cleanly. The opposition may not push until the ball comes in and are going to move the scrum back in any case so there is no difference. An added bonus if a man is missing is that the men not in the scrum are ready to defend against moves designed to expose the lack of a flank forward.

While not advocating these ploys for every team they are worth considering should the situation arise.

Positional Play in the Scrum

Although this is not intended as a highly technical coaching manual and it is not intended to get involved in foot positions and technique it is worth looking at the function of individual positions in the scrum. These involve preparation off the practice field to make oneself able to carry out the wishes of the coach.

Prop

The main job is to transmit the push of the rest of the scrum. It is not a pleasant feeling to be pushed extremely hard from the back and front and obviously strength in the back is most important. If this strength is not there the whole scrum will cease to be effective. Very often teams are prepared to sacrifice full participation in other aspects of the game for this one quality.

Hooker

The main task is to get the ball but there are other important functions. First the good hooker will evolve a technique which does not disrupt his own side's scrummaging. The eel-like hooker may be very impressive in getting balls against the head but he can cause right moves for his props who are trying to retain positions which will transmit the push of the rest of the scrum.

The second and almost always forgotten task is to become another pusher as soon as the ball is struck. This helps to counter the eight men which the opposition might be using to push against you.

Second Row

The second row must be the powerhouse of the scrum. As the core they must be particularly tightly bound. They are nearly always the biggest men on the field and therefore not very mobile, and so they must use all their weight to advantage.

No. 8

As with the second row the No. 8 is able to push his full weight with both shoulders in contact and must lock them together while driving as powerfully as he can.

Flankers

They can add more weight than is often accepted and are vital in locking the front row solidly together. They should push slightly in to prevent the props being pushed out by the second rows (*see* Fig. 1).

CHAPTER EIGHT

The Ruck and the Maul

To play good rugby a team must be able to win rucks and mauls. It is possible to win matches by winning scrums and kicking, but rugby is the great game it is at its best because of its continuity. Thus when a man is tackled the game must not stop, and it is here that the skills of rucking and mauling come in. From a set scrum or a line-out both sides are lined up waiting for each other. Although clear set moves can create opportunities direct from this situation, it is more likely that they will give one side an attacking edge which must then be exploited. Winning the ruck and maul which follows will often produce a situation with a decisive advantage to the attacking side because the opposition has been committed. This makes it more likely that tries will result and good rugby must involve by scoring.

The New Zealand sides of the 1960s were the best ruckers and maulers we have seen in recent years and even though some of their back play was not as imaginative as it might have been, they produced so much ball for them that they were prolific try scorers. People often talk about this aspect of the game as winning 'second-phase ball' the 'first phase' being the scrum or line-out which is a set play awarded by the referee. The great difference between the two is that nobody has a set position in a ruck or maul, and every player, including the three-quarters, must be able to take part if the situation requires.

The perfect ruck would look the same as a set scrum (and that is why it is often known as a loose scrum) but the difference is that the front row could be the back row or even the centres. If they stand out and wait for the front row to arrive the opposition will have won the ball long before.

The maul will look similar but the ball is not on the ground but held firmly and safely out of reach of the opposition.

The pictures on page 48 in the Line-out chapter are valid for the maul as well as the line-out. Everything is perfect for the rest of the forwards to drive Sutherland and his support and drag in the opposition.

The ball is released only when the scrum-half thinks the moment is right. The advantage of the maul over the ruck is that the ball is in the hand and therefore more under control than when on the floor.

Any chapter on rucking and mauling is really an extension of 'Physical Contact' because it is invariably the actions of the first people to the maul that decide whether it will be won or lost or will remain inconclusive and cause yet another scrum.

If a ruck follows a tackle the best technique in the world will not release the ball if the tackled player has put

himself between his own forwards and the ball.

This is why it is so important to try and remain standing. It is much easier to retain any advantage gained in that position than on the ground. Although it is quite possible to 'kill' the ball in a standing position it happens more frequently when a player from the side not likely to win it throws himself on

Rugby Union

top of it. Various players have perfected different techniques to make sure that the ball can be released when opposition hands threaten to prevent its release.

Ian McLachlan, the diminutive 'Mighty Mouse', perfected a technique where he pushed it back through his legs while still driving forward. This was effective because he was close to the ground and prepared to put his hand almost to the floor to protect the ball.

Brian Thomas, the massive Welsh lock of the 1960s, would just force himself down to the ground with the ball turning as he did so. Such was his weight that no player succeeded in keeping a hold on the ball and it always popped out on

the right side.

Mike Roberts, another man with enormous strength, begins to buck like a fighting bull and often succeeds in lifting opposition and ball out of the top of a maul.

Upon being tackled the player will often be forced to the ground and therefore has to release the ball. It is the next man who must try to regain control of it and make himself strong to release it to his own support thus forming the core to the maul.

However, it is important that forming the maul does not become the aim of the game – again the All Blacks in the 1960s seemed to over-emphasise this technique. If it is possible to move in after a tackle, secure the ball, and move it away without a maul then this should be done. There is of course an exception to this. If the opposition are strung out right across the field it might be better to form a maul to draw them in and create more space in which to move once the ball is won.

The part played by the three-quarters cannot be stressed too much. Very often a three-quarters cannot be the first person to a breakdown and he must be prepared to move in and secure the ball. If he cannot do it alone it might well be that other backs can help him. Three-quarters often argue that if they do not succeed in winning the ball they are in no position to defend but this argument does not really stand up when we are thinking about winning. It should only make them more determined to get in quickly and ensure possession. Each three-quarter is first of all a player and only secondly a fly-half or wing.

CHAPTER NINE

The Half-backs

Although there have undoubtedly been many great scrum-halves and fly-halves down through the ages of rugby, it is usually a half-back pairing which springs readily to mind when reminiscing and analysing. Edwards and John, Willis and Morgan, Hawthorn and Catchpole (Australia), Jeeps and Sharp are pairings which have thrilled the world by their superb understanding and skill as a pair, coupled nevertheless with a retention of individual flair.

It is necessary to examine not only the roles of the scrum-half and fly-half separately, but also their role in partnership. The individual attributes of a scrum-half may differ considerably from those of a fly-half, and yet if the two are completely incompatible and fail to strike up any code of understanding then the consequences could be disastrous for the team irrespective of the individual skills.

The half-backs are regarded essentially as the link between the forwards and the three-quarters. For many years forwards were thought of simply as ball-getters or ball-winners, whereas the three-quarters were the try-scorers. While each of these positions retains much of that

description, there is now, in the modern game, considerably more overlap of each group's role. This has in turn placed greater onus on the half-backs, and the more important the game, the heavier is the burden of responsibility on them.

The importance of understanding and unity between scrum-half and fly-half can never be over-estimated, and yet, before that, each individual must possess skill of a certain level. Obviously, the higher the level of individual skill, the better the half-back partnership will be. The two players, while so essentially compatible, are players possessing different skills, and seldom is an interchange of positions a realistic item.

The physical demands on a scrum-half are such that he must be strong and courageous, because these two qualities will frequently be tested by the big, strong and heavy forwards in the opposition. This does not imply that the fly-half must be less strong or indifferent in his approach, but rather that the scrum-half is far more exposed to the physical side of the game. The skills required by each may differ considerably. Whereas the earlier chapters dealt with the individual skills that ought to be the

Rugby Union

armoury of *all* players, there are certain situations within a game which call upon the special skills of a scrum- or fly-half.

In the match itself there are usually something approaching forty to fifty scrums, of which it is reasonable to assume that one particular scrum-half will put the ball into the scrum 50 per cent of the time. The practice of putting the ball into the scrum accurately is a difficult one, and the laws governing the feed-in are quite strict. This thus necessitates a great deal of practice between scrum-half and hooker and the other seven forwards. The art of good scrummaging has been covered in another chapter, but the relationship that exists between scrum-half and forwards is one that must be practised over and over again if the scrummage is going to be a platform from which to launch an attack. Yet the inconsistency in scrum feeding can nullify all the hours of hard weight-training and practice. To exemplify this point then watch a team that loses its regular scrum-half through injury at the very next scrummage.

The scrum-half's primary concern at a set scrummage is, more often than not, to pass the ball safely and accurately into the eager arms of his fly-half. Once that has been achieved the scrum-half, briefly at least, is satisfied. With the ball in the fly-half's hands the problem is 'what to do next ?' The fly-half in practices might be the best catcher, passer and kicker of the ball in the whole club, let alone team, but he now receives the ball in a realistic game situation.

This brings in a new facet of the game — pressure from the opposition. Can the fly-half, armed with his technical individual skills, choose the tactic that the situation demands ?

Of course, once the fly-half receives the 'good' ball from his scrum-half, then the decision he makes is greatly influenced by the calibre of the three-quarters outside him, both individually and collectively. For many years in Wales, for example, the fly-half was reluctant to pass on the ball in case something 'went wrong' ! Fortunately, the better organisation that coaching has brought has dispelled these fears and the result has certainly benefited the game.

Furthermore, whereas in the past the fly-half was the 'prima donna' of the team and seldom called upon to tackle or be tackled, the three-quarter line as a defensive unit now places a great deal of reliance upon the defensive qualities of the fly-half. With the role of flanker changing (due in no small way to the change in the laws) then greater onus is placed upon the fly-half to tackle — and in many cases if he does not the defensive wall is breached, and those rather large forwards pile through the hole.

While, in essence, therefore, the roles of scrum- and fly-half have not changed whether as individuals or as a pair, they have developed into a unit which must work very closely with the other units in the team, i.e. with the forwards and the three-quarters.

CHAPTER TEN

Three-quarter Play

Most players at the very beginning of their rugby careers quite understandably model themselves on a top international player. It is not surprising to find that more often than not that player is a member of the three-quarters line or perhaps more frequently a half-back. These days every budding rugby player wants to be a Barry John, a Mike Gibson, a David Duckham, a Gerald Davies or a John Williams. The reason behind this is quite simple – these people play in positions which allow them to show their tremendous flair, skill and speed and therefore they offer the most excitement. Of these great players I have particular admiration for Michael Gibson because his technical ability is unsurpassed by any other player in the world. The illustrations which appear earlier in the book exemplify this.

Each three-quarter position has special skills peculiar to it. All of these players mentioned are of the highest class and yet lose some of their effectiveness when they play out of position which only serves to show that a player must learn his positional play more thoroughly than just mastering the skills he will use.

For example, the fine All Black wing Bryan Williams is a world-class left-wing but some of his effectiveness is lost when he is transferred to the right, and the same player placed in midfield is almost unrecognisable. This is borne out by a comparison of his performances when he played left-wing for the World XV against England in 1971 to his performances at centre against the 1971 Lions and his most recent appearances as right-wing for the All Blacks during their 1973 tours.

The game these days is highly technical and far more tactical than ever before. Subsequently players with innate ability must not only be selected and played in their most effective position but those players alongside must be ever-increasingly aware of their ability, and must work for their partners by setting up situations where they can show their strength. A team must therefore see the need for a well-balanced three-quarter unit and not a group of individuals who, inspite of their skill, are unable to blend into a match-winning combination. Because of coaching, greater dedication from players, and changes in the laws of the

Rugby Union

game, teams have become much stronger in defence thus making it more difficult for the three-quarter line to penetrate. It is, and always has been, desirable for those players with natural running ability to be given the ball 'with room to move'. A close look at the game shows that this is in the wing positions, which automatically means that the people inside – the midfield men – must fulfil roles of 'link men'. In order to do so effectively, they must be extremely proficient in the basic skills – perhaps even more than the player they are trying to feed ! This, of course, requires a great deal of practice and this has certainly been stressed throughout the book.

If it is accepted that the winger has most room in which to move (assuming he has been properly supplied), then in modern rugby football, another player pursues an important role in seeking to achieve this end. That player, of course, is the full-back and there can be no greater exponent of attacking full-back play than John Williams of London Welsh and Wales. Although it was the change in the laws in the late sixties which made the full-back a necessary attacker, it was J. P. R. Williams who showed its enormous potential. Quite a large proportion of J.P.R.'s success was due to his physical size, strength and speed which made him a dangerous player in his own right but his greatest attribute to a three-quarter line was his sense of timing – how and where he was going to burst into the line. While some of it was his uncanny reading of a game, most of it had been worked out and rehearsed on the training field. He,

himself, would readily admit that the confidence derived from practising a move made him all the more eager to use it. Players of much less ability than John Williams can be effective provided they, together with the other members of the three-quarter line, are able and willing to practise as a unit.

In dealing with this one aspect of three-quarter play, one must not fall into the trap of thinking that this is the only role of a back line incorporating the full-back. Many teams suffer because this particular pattern of play is the only one attempted, and it becomes predictable and totally ineffective. The attributes required by each of the individual members of the three-quarter line are no different to those required since rugby first began. The great difference now is that the three-quarter line, indeed the entire back division, must be seen as a complete unit and seen to operate as such, making the maximum use of the skills of each individual. There is the obvious danger that too many set moves, however well rehearsed and executed, will stifle the flair of the individual because they are over-emphasised and over-used.

A further aspect of three-quarter play which formed one of the foundation stones for the success of the 1971 British Lions was the communication – during an actual game – between forwards and backs. The first hurdle for any three-quarter is to cross the 'gain-line', but very often many moves peter out or scoring opportunities are lost because of lack of adequate support. Forwards cry out to be told what is going to happen at the next line-out or scrum and while 'King' Barry John would not tell the forwards anything at all in case they got in the way, it is not unreasonable to tell them in which direction the attack is to be launched. At least, then, they can have no excuse for getting in the way!!

Very often when a strongly defensive three-quarter line stops a more powerfully attacking one, it is the element of surprise, coupled with the unexpected flair of the individual, which tears defenses to shreds. Yet it is the badly executed move or the error on the part of the individual which brings most frustrations – especially to the forwards – and this can not be entirely eliminated but certainly reduced to a minimum by constant practice.

There are many moves which are used by many different three-quarter lines, for example, the scissors, the dummy scissors, the loop-around, the missing out of a man with a pass, etc. But those which stand most chance of succeeding are those which are simple to understand and execute when under the sustained pressure of a game. The more complicated a particular move becomes, the more likely it is to break down.

The lessons of three-quarter play, therefore, can be summarised as follows:

(a) Make the best use of individual flair;
(b) Act and think as a unit in all situations;
(c) Practise as individuals and as a unit.

CHAPTER ELEVEN

The Game

Rugby has now emerged as one of the most exciting contact sports in the world. Its popularity is growing so that it is becoming a truly international game. This was not always so. For a long time it was regarded (or disregarded) by the uninitiated as a strange game appreciated only by the aficionados. It almost always seemed so stilted that they were quite happy to leave them to it. Several factors have changed the game and there is no doubt that it has changed enormously over the last decade. There have been two important law changes which have given the game greater continuity.

(1) A player no longer has to play the ball with his foot after a tackle ;
(2) A player may no longer kick the ball directly into touch from outside his own 25-yard line except from a penalty.

These law changes mean that the ball is in the hand far more and as rugby is essentially a running and handling game they have helped to make it more of a spectacle. They have also made it a simpler and more enjoyable game to play which has increased the number of people participating.

However, it is still a very complex game and one of the greatest drawbacks in the development of rugby was the attitude towards practice and coaching. The old adage 'We play rugby to get fit, we don't get fit to play rugby' was all too true. It has been the changing of this attitude which has had the greatest effect.

It is impossible to play for fun if that fun is ruined for the individual and the rest of the team because of frustration which builds up when movements break down because of lack of skill. Many of the skills in rugby are unnatural and therefore require even more practice than skills in other sports. For example, it is totally unnatural to run forward and be required to pass backwards. It is perhaps because there is so much frustration on the field that rugby players have such a reputation for having their fun in the bar.

In other countries there has not been the same reluctance to accept coaching and it was the constant beatings at the hands of New Zealand and South Africa which helped to speed up the acceptance of it in the few home countries. Well-coached All Black and Springbok teams ruled the rugby world for many years and it was not until 1971 that a British Lions Touring team managed to win a series against either. It has to be more than coincidence that the position of British rugby in the world is higher than ever before. Now the coach is rightfully an important man and good coaches are at a premium. Nearly all clubs have a coach and those that do not would like one but cannot find the right man. In a club such as London Welsh there is a coach for each team. Because rugby is an amateur game the time a coach can spend with his team is limited and it is important that that time is not wasted. Carwyn James, who masterminded the victories of the 1971 Lions, always used to say that fitness was the responsibility of the individual and that a player had to be fit enough to take one of his practice sessions. He felt that it was a waste of his expertise to concentrate on anything but the game. Too many coaches still have to spend most of their time getting players fit instead of coaching. It is not a coach's job to make a prop strong enough to be able to play in his position properly. This should be done before the season starts and would probably require a weight-training programme through the close season.

Having established that coaching is now accepted and desirable it would be wrong to look upon it as the answer to all problems. It brings with it some very real dangers which can have a very bad effect on the game. A bad coach can eliminate flair and so dominate his players that they become automatons ready to do his will. This will gradually lead to less enjoyment and the whole situation has gone full cycle.

It is, therefore, important for the individual to make sure that he has his own philosophy about the way in which he wishes to play the game. This will, of course, be influenced by the coach but it should always come through in the course of a game. Barry John was a great example. However disciplined a role he was asked to play he always found an opportunity to show his almost arrogant confidence in toying with the opposition.

The other great worry is that 'winning' will become too important. Everybody likes to win and a game not played for victory is pointless but the way that victory is achieved is also very important. Full enjoyment of the game demands that the game be played in the right spirit and with the right aims. It should be possible to come off the field having lost and yet feeling that the game was enjoyable – it should also be possible to feel totally dissatisfied with a game which has been won because your team did not play well by your own standards.

There is no doubt that standards have improved in the last decade because of coaching and the organisation which goes with it. Players are more aware of the roles of other players and their own role within the team as a whole. (This is not to say that some of the great players of the past would not be just as great today. In fact Cliff Morgan, Jeff Butterfield and Tony O'Reilly might well have been even more devastating with the rest of the team working to set them up.)

However, the game still relies upon exactly the same basic skills as before. A powerful pack can dominate a game